COLOUR US BACK

FROM HISTORY

(WOMEN)

A colouring book of important female personalities

ELLE SMITH

COLOUR US BACK FROM HISTORY (WOMEN)

The information contained in 'Colour Us Back from History (Women)', and its components, is meant to serve for information purposes only, as researched by the author.

The author has made all reasonable efforts to provide current and accurate information for the readers of this book. The author and associates will not be held liable for any errors, unintentional or otherwise, or omissions that may be found.

The material in this book may include information from third parties. Third party materials include opinions expressed by their owners, and as such the author of this book does not assume responsibility or accept any liability for third party material or opinions.

Whether because of the progression of the Internet, or the unforeseen changes in company policy and editorial submission guidelines, what is stated as a fact at the time of this writing may become outdated or inapplicable later.

Published 2018 by Inspired By Elle (Publishing), United Kingdom

www.inspiredbyelle.com

All Rights Reserved

Copyright © 2018 Elle Smith

The right of Elle Smith to be identified as the author of this work has been asserted in accordance with section 77 and 78 of the Copyright Designs and Patents Act 1988.

This book is copyright © 2018 Elle Smith with all rights reserved. It is sold under condition that it shall not, by way of trade or otherwise, be lent, re-sold, hired out or otherwise circulated in any other form of binding or cover other than that in which it is published and without a similar condition including this condition being imposed on the subsequent purchaser(s).

It is illegal to redistribute, copy, or create derivative works from this book whole or in parts. No parts of this book may be photocopied or reproduced in any form or electronically (or otherwise), stored in any retrieval system, or transmitted in any way without the prior permission of the publisher.

ISBN: 978-1-9999023-4-6

TABLE OF CONTENTS

INTRODUCTION 5

MILDRED S. DRESSELHAUS 7

HELLEN KELLER 11

DOROTHY DANDRIDGE 15

MAE CAROL JEMISON 19

MARY SEACOLE 23

HEDY LAMARR 27

NELLIE BLY 31

ELIZABETH JENNINGS GRAHAM 34

VERA LASKA 37

ELIZABETH GARRETT ANDERSON 41

A NOTE FROM THE AUTHOR: 45

INTRODUCTION

History is a record of vast amounts of information and as is usually the case with voluminous pieces of information, some parts are remembered more than others. There are many reasons to justify why we need to remember the past. Indeed, history is filled with important deeds performed by great people and these deeds have brought us to where we are right now.

We, as humans, have a moral and ethical obligation to preserve the stories of certain people and in some cases, amplify them so they receive the recognition they truly deserve.

Knowledge of history is especially important now that we live in the internet age which has been characterized by a monumental shift away from books and the danger exists therefore, that we may forget and consequently, repeat mistakes of the past.

I like to think that "we cannot birth a better tomorrow if we do not know what we did in the past" and so I wrote this two-part series of books of notable people, not only from the distant past, whom I believe have not been given enough credit for their achievements.

There are currently two books featuring men and women from history, who may not have received the recognition they deserved. Each of the respective books feature ten men and ten women. Both books have beautiful drawings of the personalities included and they can be coloured in as a fun activity by both adults and children. The aim being to literally colour these characters back into significance, while you learn about the personalities at the same time.

I hope you learn a lot from this book and have some fun while relaxing to colour the images back into your history.

Elle Smith

Colour Us Back From History (Women)

1. MILDRED S. DRESSELHAUS

●●●

BIOGRAPHY

Mildred Dresselhaus was born Mildred Spiewak on 11 November 1930 to Polish-Jewish parents in Brooklyn and grew up in the Bronx during the Great Depression. Her talent for music brought her in contact with richer families that encouraged her to pursue an education. Dresselhaus, who was already interested in science after encountering several old issues of *National Geographic,* subsequently attended Hunter High in New York City. She went on to Hunter College where she got her first degree in 1951 and was encouraged by future Nobel laureate Rosalyn Yalow to go to graduate school to study physics.

Dresselhaus took post graduate science classes at Harvard but because of segregation rules at the time, she had to take her classes separate from men. Undeterred, she went on to get her master's degree from Radcliffe College in 1953.

In 1958, she got her PhD from the University of Chicago and married Gene Dresselhaus, a well-known theoretician and discoverer of the Dresselhaus effect. The Dresselhaus effect is a phenomenon in condensed matter physics in which spin-orbit interaction within a particle causes energy bands to split. The couple had a family comprising of four children born between 1959 and 1964.

Mildred Dresselhaus's research began in earnest after her PhD and she took positions at Cornell University and the Lincoln Laboratory before moving to the Massachusetts Institute of Technology ("MIT") in 1967.

She arrived as a visiting professor of physics and within months, was offered a permanent position. She immediately delved into graphite intercalation, where she studied and created materials in which graphite alternated with other species in atom-thick sheets. It is this technology that is responsible for objects such as lithium-ion batteries and nanocarbons.

By 1983, Dresselhaus was a professor of electrical engineering and in 1985, she became the first female Institute Professor at the prestigious MIT. She continued to research and pioneer discoveries in graphite, fullerenes, spin-orbit coupling, low-dimensional thermoelectrics and carbon nanotubes.

The work done by Mildred Dresselhaus helped develop technology that worked on thin graphite and has allowed electronics to be utilised in practically everything around us from clothing to smartphones. Dresselhaus has been given numerous honours and awards including the National Medal of Science (she was in fact the first woman to receive it), the Enrico Fermi award and the Presidential Medal of Freedom.

Dresselhaus, who was widely applauded for encouraging and inspiring women to take up careers in science, was fondly known as the "Queen of Carbon" and passed away on 20 February 2017.

Fun Fact

In 1992, both the navies of the U.S.A and France asked her to help them design a new power system capable of shielding them from Russian detection.

Notable Quote

"Some people don't like competition but competition is fine. It generates new ideas and keeps you alert."

MILDRED DRESSELHAUS

2. HELLEN KELLER

•••

BIOGRAPHY

Helen Adams Keller (27 June 1880 – 1 June 1968) was born in Tuscumbia, Alabama. She developed quickly, beginning to speak at 6 months and walking at 1 year old. She was born with her full senses of sight and hearing but in 1882, around 19 months of age, she was struck with an illness that eventually left her blind and deaf. This illness was described as "brain fever" by doctors, which even today cannot be properly pinpointed, although many medical practitioners believe it might have been scarlet fever or meningitis.

Her blindness and deafness made her isolated in her home and the person with whom she communicated the most, was Martha Washington, the daughter of the family cook. She knew a few signs but her communication remained limited. Helen started to express her frustration with wild tantrums, placing her family under great strain.

Keller's parents finally took her to the Perkins Institute for the Blind in Boston, Massachusetts where one of the school's recent graduates, Anne Sullivan was recommended. In March 1887, Sullivan moved to the Alabama home of the Kellers and began to work directly teaching young Helen.

Initially, there was hardly any improvement, mostly due to Helen's defiance and wild temper. Even when Helen attempted to learn, she found it difficult to grasp the relationships between distinct words and signs, so was easily frustrated. Anne took the measure of isolating young Helen Keller and herself in a cottage, which gave rise to a breakthrough as Keller began to properly sign words. Anne Sullivan remained Helen's companion for the next 49 years.

Helen Keller then began to undergo formal education between 1888 and 1898. She attended several special schools including the Perkins Institute for the Blind and the Horace Mann School for the Deaf.

In 1900, she gained admission to Radcliffe College at Harvard University and graduated in 1904, becoming the first deaf and blind person to get a Bachelor of Arts degree. Helen Keller was determined to communicate as much as possible, and so she learned how to speak along with other forms of communication including touch-lip reading, Braille, typing and finger spelling.

Keller went on to become a world-famous speaker and advocate for people with disabilities, travelling to at least 25 countries. She also identified as a socialist, pacifist, birth control supporter and women's right activist. Notably, as a member of the Socialist Party, she wrote and campaigned for better rights for the working class. She helped to found the American Civil Liberties Union, and joined the Industrial Workers of the World, as part of her social activism.

Helen Keller went on to publish 12 books and several articles. She is a recipient of numerous awards including the Presidential Medal of Freedom and is a member of the National Women's Hall of Fame.

Fun Fact

Helen Keller won an Oscar for a documentary about her life.

Notable Quote

"Life is either a great adventure or nothing."

HELEN KELLER

3. DOROTHY DANDRIDGE

•••

BIOGRAPHY

Dorothy Dandridge (9 November 1922 – 8 September 1965) was an iconic actress in film and theatre as well as a singer and dancer. She was born in Cleveland, Ohio to her actress mother, Ruby Dandridge, who separated from her husband just before Dorothy's birth. Consequently, Dorothy never knew her father.

Ruby created a song and dance act for her two daughters and while she worked in Cleveland, Dorothy and her sister, Vivian, toured most of the south. As a result of the Great Depression, bookings became scarce for the whole family and they ended up moving to Hollywood in 1930. Eventually, the sister act began to get gigs again, notably in Harlem, New York at venues like The Cotton Club and the Apollo Theatre.

Dorothy soon encountered segregation and racism. She was not allowed to eat in certain restaurants, even at venues where she had just gone on stage.

Her career began to pick up in early 1935, when Dorothy started to get small uncredited roles in film, sometimes as part of the sister act with Vivian and sometimes by herself. Throughout the 1940s, with her film career not really taking off, Dorothy Dandridge continued to perform as a singer.

She got married to Harold Nicholas, a dancer, in 1942; the union was mostly unhappy but produced a daughter called Harolyn.

In 1951, after her divorce and appearances in supporting roles like *Tarzan's Peril* (which was considered a provocative delight), and *The Harlem Globetrotters,* she was approached by Metro Goldwyn Mayer to star in *Bright Road* alongside Harry Belafonte. The movie was a hit. That same year, her singing at the Mocambo club in Hollywood became hugely successful, leading to international bookings.

In 1953, she got the lead role in the movie, *Carmen Jones* which was a worldwide success and was one of the most profitable movies that year. This movie is probably considered as her defining moment as an actress.

Dorothy Dandridge's role in Carmen Jones earned her an Academy Award nomination for best actress, making her the first African-American to be nominated. Dorothy Dandridge never really re-enacted the success of Carmen Jones because racial stereotyping made it difficult for her to find great roles.

Her last great work is considered to be *Porgy and Bess* where she starred opposite Sidney Poitier and earned a Golden Globe nomination for best actress in a musical.

She took on a few international productions and continued to perform on the nightclub circuit until her death in 1965.

Fun Fact

Although the director originally considered Dorothy's looks as too sophisticated for the part, she got the role for Carmen Jones by radically altering her clothes and changing her makeup.

Notable Quote

"There is no force more powerful than a woman determined to rise."

Colour Us Back From History (Women)

4. MAE CAROL JEMISON

●●●

BIOGRAPHY

Mae Carol Jemison was born in Decatur, Alabama on 17 October 1956. Her family moved to Chicago when she was 3 years old. It was in this location that her interest in science blossomed. She was also interested in dancing and at the age of 14, earned a role in the *West Side Story* play.

Jemison graduated from Morgan Park High School in 1973 at the age of 16 years, and gained a place at Stanford University. She experienced racial discrimination even from her professors but she was determined to get her degree. In 1977, she graduated from Stanford with a degree in Chemical Engineering. While at Stanford, she continued to fan her interest in the arts, choreographing a dance production and fulfilling the requirements for a Batchelor of Arts in African and Afro-American Studies.

Jemison's career seemed at a crossroads but she continued academia by attending medical school, realizing she could still dance if she wanted. She practised medicine for a while after her graduation in 1981, and later joined the Peace Corps.

Jemison applied to join NASA after the flight of Sally Ride in 1983, but there was a delay due to a program overhaul within NASA after a space shuttle accident in 1986. She re-applied in 1987 and was accepted.

Jemison worked at NASA coordinating launch support and verifying Shuttle computer software before her big break. This came in 1992 when she flew on space mission STS-47 as a Mission Specialist, becoming the first African American woman to travel in space.

In 1993, Mae Jemison resigned from NASA to explore her interest in the relationship between technology and social science, especially how technology affects everyday lives.

Later that year she founded the Jemison Group, a company that researches, and develops science technology for application in daily life.

In 1999, she founded BioSentient Corporation, a company working on mobile devices capable of monitoring the autonomic (or involuntary) nervous system. In 2012, her foundation won a grant from the government to work on the 100 Year Starship Project.

Mae Jemison has written a few books, continues to work on her companies, and still organizes dance productions.

Fun Fact

Mae Jemison appeared in an episode of *Star Trek: The Next Generation*, becoming the first real life astronaut to be on the show.

Notable Quote

"Never limit yourself because of others' limited imagination."

MAE CAROL JEMISON

Colour Us Back From History (Women)

5. MARY SEACOLE

• • •

BIOGRAPHY

Mary Seacole (23 November 1805 – 14 May 1881) was born Mary Jane Grant in Kingston, Jamaica. Her father was a Scottish Lieutenant in the British army; and her mother was a Jamaican traditional healer, from whom she learned traditional African and Caribbean medicine. She lived at the home of an elderly woman for some time and received a good education.

She travelled to London to visit some of her relatives in 1821, and ended up staying for almost a year. Later, on her return home, she helped out at her mother's boarding house, Blundell Hall, and assisted at the British Army hospital.

She widely travelled the Caribbean and returned to Jamaica, where she married Edward Seacole in 1836. She managed Blundell Hall for several years after losing both her mother and husband in 1844. Seacole successfully treated cholera patients in the Jamaican epidemic of 1850. She similarly treated patients in 1851, while visiting her half brother in Panama.

On her travels, she picked up vast knowledge of Western medicine and added that to her repertoire of traditional medicine.

After the Crimean War broke out in late 1853, Mary Seacole decided to travel to England to volunteer as a nurse at the War Office. Despite being rejected, she resolved to travel on her own to the Crimean peninsula. She established the British Hotel near Balaclava on her arrival, and took care of many sick or recovering officers, who had been afflicted by war injuries and cholera.

Seacole returned to England in 1856 after the war ended, and found her finances in a terrible state. However several officers and royalty who had been impressed with her loyal work in

Crimea, arranged a fundraiser to stabilize her situation. Mary Seacole subsequently published her autobiography in 1857, and it was a huge success.

Mary Seacole travelled back to Jamaica in 1860, returned to England in 1870 and passed away in her London home in 1881.

Fun Fact

Mary Seacole was known as "The Creole with the Tea Mug" because she always brought beverages for the soldiers.

Notable Quote

"Beside the nettle, ever grows the cure for its sting."

MARY SEACOLE

Colour Us Back From History (Women)

6. HEDY LAMARR

•••

BIOGRAPHY

Hedy Lamarr (9 November 1914 – 19 January 2000) was born Hedwig Eva Maria Kiesler in Vienna. Her career started as a script girl before she became an actress. She successfully landed the lead role in Gustav Machaty's *Ecstasy* at the tender age of 18 years in 1933. This movie contained some close-up nude scenes, which was an uncommon 'concept' at the time.

Although the movie was frowned upon in the United States, it was celebrated throughout Europe as a work of art and was given an award in Italy. Still, Hedy was dismayed because the director had misled her into thinking the nude scenes would not have visible details.

She stuck to stage productions and married one of her admirers, Friedrich Mandl. Mandl had ties to Mussolini and the Nazis; thus it was at meetings discussing military technology, that Hedy picked up an interest in applied science.

Mandl, who heavily disapproved of the *Ecstasy* movie, tried to control her and she realized her career would never flourish if she remained married to him. This led to her fleeing to Paris in 1937; where she met Louis B. Mayer of Metro Goldwyn Mayer. He advised her to change her name to Hedy Lamarr because she was known at the time as "The Ecstasy Lady", and the name change would allow her career to renew.

Her first Hollywood movie, *Algiers,* released in 1938 was a "national sensation" and Lamarr's career quickly escalated as people queued to watch her striking good looks as she delivered strong performances.

Eventually, she began to be typecast in Hollywood and in her free time, the self-taught Lamarr worked on scientific hobbies and inventions. She sketched ideas based on her study of birds and shared them with aviation businessman Howard Hughes who had been reviewing how to make his planes fly faster. During World War II, she had an idea to prevent torpedoes from being jammed. She contacted her friend George Antheil, and together, they designed a device with a frequency-hopping system. The design was patented in 1942.

The design was unused because the U.S. Navy was reluctant to try ideas coming from outside the military. During the Cuban missile crisis in 1962, the Navy began to use an updated version of the design.

Lamarr also worked with Antheil on spread spectrum technology and it is considered a precursor to technologies like Bluetooth, Wi-Fi and GPS.

Fun Fact

Hedy Lamarr invented an improved traffic stoplight.

Notable Quotes

"Analysis gave me great freedom of emotions and fantastic confidence. I felt I had served my time as a puppet."

HEDY LAMARR

Colour Us Back From History (Women)

7. NELLIE BLY

•••

BIOGRAPHY

The journalist and author known as Nellie Bly was born Elizabeth Jane Cochran on 5 May 1864. In her teenage years, she changed her surname to "Cochrane" because it sounded more sophisticated. Even though her father was rich, (their town was named after him), he died without a will and so many of his children from his two wives had little money to support themselves.

After graduating from Indiana Normal School, Elizabeth attended college briefly before dropping out due to financial constraints. Sometime in 1882, at the tender age of 18 years, she responded brilliantly to an editorial piece that declared that women were only fit for domestic duties. This response earned her a job at the paper, the Pittsburgh Dispatch, and it was here that she took on the pen name "Nellie Bly" after a popular song of the period. (She intended to use "Nelly" but her editor mistakenly spelled it as "Nellie" and the name stuck).

Sadly her career stalled seemingly as she was only assigned to women's pages. She moved to Mexico and spent about six months as a foreign correspondent. Her experiences during this posting, were later turned into a book, aptly titled "*Six Months in Mexico.*"

In 1887, she moved to New York and took a job at Joseph Pulitzer's New York World. One of her first assignments was an undercover job where she pretended to be insane and spent ten days at an asylum. Her reports about brutality and neglect of the patients became famous and led to extensive reforms. Her experiences were made into a book, "*Ten Days in a Mad-House*". She later also conducted investigative work on factories, jails and the state legislature.

In 1888, Nellie Bly took a trip around the world, inspired by Jules Verne's *Around the World in 80 days.* Her trip was a success and she completed it in 72 days, a world record at the time.

She married millionaire industrialist Robert Seaman in 1895 at the age of 31, and after his death in 1904, ran the company, giving her employees splendid social benefits. Under her watch, the company began to manufacture the standard steel drum still used in the United States today.

Nellie Bly passed away in 1922.

Fun Fact

Nellie Bly successfully patented an improved milk can and a stacking garbage can.

Notable Quote

"Energy rightly applied and directed will accomplish anything."

ELIZABETH COCHRANE SEAMAN
(aka Nellie Bly)

8. ELIZABETH JENNINGS GRAHAM

●●●

BIOGRAPHY

This teacher and civil rights figure was born "free" in New York between 1826 and 1830 (sources differ). Slavery had been abolished at the time, but New York was still heavily segregated. Her parents were important members of the African-American community and Elizabeth was raised to value education and the church, where she became the organist.

Notably in 1854, Elizabeth was told to get off a streetcar and she refused. After getting into an altercation with the streetcar conductor, a policeman was called in and Elizabeth was pushed off. She decided to sue the company operating the streetcar, and won the lawsuit. It was a huge event in the history of civil rights, even though it took about 20 years more for segregation on New York streetcars to end.

She married Charles Graham in 1860 and after the deaths of husband Charles and her son, Thomas, only a few years later, she turned the first floor of her home into the first kindergarten for black children in the city.

Elizabeth Jennings Graham passed away in 1901.

Fun Fact

At the lawsuit against the streetcar company, Elizabeth was represented by Chester Arthur, who would go on to become a U.S. president.

Notable Quote

"I am a respectable person."

ELIZABETH JENNINGS GRAHAM

Colour Us Back From History (Women)

9. VERA LASKA

•••

BIOGRAPHY

Vera Laska was born Vera Oravec in Kosice, Czechoslovakia on 21 July 1923. Growing up, she considered pursuing a career in professional athletics then teaching but World War II changed everything in her life.

She was devastated when the German Army occupied her country. She was especially horrified at the treatment handed out to Jews as she had many friends in the Jewish community. In 1938, when she was only 15, she unwittingly joined the resistance with a friend when they used their expert skiing skills to lead two men from Slovakia to Hungary.

She then joined the resistance fully and over the next few years, led multiple trips to evacuate political and Jewish refugees. She successfully eluded the Nazis for several years, but was eventually arrested with false papers in early 1943. Some accounts say she escaped this arrest, but surrendered when her mother was arrested and taken to Auschwitz. Her mother was reportedly gassed on the day Vera arrived at Auschwitz. She became part of a cooking club with other women to sustain morale and in 1944, took on an assignment at a textile factory in Gross-Rosen.

Here, Vera and other workers subtly engaged in slowdown strikes and other acts of sabotage against Nazi soldiers. In early 1945, when she was transferred to the Dora-Mittelbau concentration camp to work on parts for the German missile programme, she sabotaged the work by mixing good parts with bad ones.

She escaped in March 1945, when the Nazis took the prisoners on a death march. She hid in a barn for four days and on the fifth day, the war ended. Vera then went back home to work at the Czech War Crime Commission while studying at Charles University. She later travelled to the United States to further her studies and met Andy Laska whom she married in 1949.

Vera Laska became a professor and authored a number of books, including some, which detailed women's efforts and resistance during the Holocaust.

Fun Fact

On some trips, Vera Laska skied with refugees from Slovakia to as far as Yugoslavia and even beyond.

Notable Quote

"I sort of slid into resistance willy-nilly."

VERA LASKA

10. ELIZABETH GARRETT ANDERSON

•••

This accomplished physician was born Elizabeth Garrett in Whitechapel, London on 9 June 1836. Her father was an entrepreneur and this meant her family moved considerably. Her early years were spent in Aldeburgh and since there was no school, she learned reading, writing and arithmetic from her mother.

At 13, she went to boarding school and after her graduation, she spent nine years at home performing domestic duties. She began training as a surgery nurse at Middlesex Hospital in 1860. However, she found herself barred from the Hospital's medical school because she was a woman, but nevertheless began to take private lessons. Other medical schools including Oxford, Glasgow and Cambridge also refused her.

In 1865, she took the medical exam and when she unexpectedly passed – with the highest marks, in fact – the Society of Apothecaries was forced to grant her a licence. Still, no hospital would employ her and so she opened her own practice which slowly but surely expanded.

In 1866, she joined the British Women's Suffrage Committee in an attempt to gain the vote for female heads of households through the legal system.

Elizabeth married James George Anderson in 1871, while continuing to push for women's inclusion in medicine and in other fields.

In her lifetime, Elizabeth Anderson was a successful female pioneer with many credits to her name including: first British woman to qualify as a physician and surgeon, first female doctor of medicine in France, first dean of a British medical school and co-founder of the first hospital staffed by women. She eventually became the mayor of Aldeburgh, making her Britain's first female mayor and magistrate.

Fun Fact

When Elizabeth Anderson heard that the University of Sorbonne in Paris was more open to female students, she taught herself French in order to study there.

Notable Quote

"I said as firmly as I could to my father, that I must have this or something else; that I could not live without some real work."

ELIZABETH GARRETT ANDERSON

Colour Us Back From History (Women)

A NOTE FROM THE AUTHOR:
WHY WE SHOULD REMEMBER HISTORICAL FIGURES

It is often easy to forget, but to forget is also dangerous. If we do not remember and celebrate the people who made important contributions to the society we have today, we stand at risk of losing touch with their essence and the lessons they taught. Ultimately, we risk losing touch with our humanity itself.

I firmly believe that so many problems in this world result from the human tendency to forget things from our past experiences. Life is a process of learning, essentially from cradle to grave. These lessons are handed down through generations to precipitate better beings for the future, and in that way to elevate humanity as a whole. We not only risk repeating those mistakes of the past, but potentially create far more catastrophic ones in the future, given the advances in technology, medicine and science. Human beings cannot cope with gaps in memory, so to ensure our proper mindfulness remains we must ensure our true history is documented and accessible.

The Colour Us Back colouring books are a collection of books which combine learning with relaxation, as you therapeutically colour back elements from our society, including people in history and even endangered animals. We can join forces to create a better tomorrow by educating ourselves on these topics. I hope you enjoy bringing the images within this book back to life in full colour, as you discover the importance of these individuals in our history.

As you have read above, I advocate for endangered animals, which I paint to highlight their plight. Please feel free to view my art paintings on my website listed below:

https://www.inspiredbyelle.com/collections/animals

I also have a YouTube channel that may be of interest to you. I encourage you to stop by and to be creatively inspired:

https://www.youtube.com/channel/UCJRn5QmZZ3vAYJ9Xv0dR5_A

Kindest,

Elle Smith

www.inspiredbyelle.com

www.ingramcontent.com/pod-product-compliance
Lightning Source LLC
Chambersburg PA
CBHW040004080526
44586CB00027B/2876